P9-DUB-610

TALKING TO STRANGERS

WITHDRAWN
UTSA Libraries

The Brittingham Prize in Poetry

The University of Wisconsin Press Poetry Series

Ronald Wallace, General Editor

TALKING TO STRANGERS

Patricia Dobler

The University of Wisconsin Press

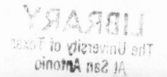
LIBRARY
The University of Texas
At San Antonio

Published 1986

The University of Wisconsin Press
114 North Murray Street
Madison, Wisconsin 53715

The University of Wisconsin Press, Ltd.
1 Gower Street
London WC1E 6HA, England

Copyright © 1986
The Board of Regents of the University of Wisconsin System
All rights reserved

First printing

Printed in the United States of America

For LC CIP information see the colophon

ISBN 0-299-10830-9 cloth, 0-299-10834-1 paper

LIBRARY
The University of Texas
At San Antonio

For Bruce

For Stephanie and Lisa

And I hope this will be counted somehow in my defense:
my regret and great longing once to express
one life, not for my glory, for a different splendor.
—Czeslaw Milosz

Contents

Foreword

One of my expectations for poetry is that it chronicle our age, for who will tell it if the poet does not? Patricia Dobler comes from immigrant Hungarian stock, men who worked in the steel mills of Ohio, a heritage rich in physical labor, some of it dangerous, all of it arduous. How this life affected the mothers and daughters, the aunts and sisters as well as the working men forms a large part of her telling. The Church, too, plays its part in what is now called character formation.

Dobler's view of her origins is free of sentimentality or idealization, but full of feeling. Images, sounds, smells, sparks of connection fly in these poems. In the opening narrative, a group of parochial schoolchildren are shepherded by their teacher along the catwalk of a steel mill: "Sister Monica understands Hell / to be like this. . . . the blazing orange heat pouring out / liquid fire like Devil's soup. . . ."

Indeed, the presence of the mill pervades the book, a haunting "black heart," "a hot breath" we feel even as we turn the pages. And these, I think, are Dobler's best poems, for they are wrung from her childhood, surfacing out of the innocent, abrupt, vivid perceptions a child has: overhearing her parents quarrel about money, then reconcile; observing the sudden prosperity World War II brings to a mill town: absorbing stories and directives from her mother, her grandmother, her aunts; and they are deeply true.

She has deftly captured the nonverbal nature of her male relatives: "When words come, you out there will hear / only the economy of their sentences." In the title poem, her father, who "all afternoon suffered his family, / the stories of their lives" in an intimacy that, we infer, was painful for him, has escaped to his ham radio set in the basement. Here he is totally at home; "he is in control" calling "CQ into the night." The poet, upstairs, watches "the herringbone pattern of his voice / on the TV: my father, talking to strangers."

There is a dignity to the protocol of ham-radio language, to these signals "homing in over the miles" and an obvious safety in their distance. What goes unsaid in the poem deepens its poignancy. Dobler exercises her poetic tact time after time, careful not to overreach, willing to let specific concrete detail carry the poem.

If these poems, infused with images of steel mill, Catholic Church, and her Hungarian ancestry, are Dobler's best, there are glimmerings of new directions in the final section of the book. Fresh strengths arise in one poem set in Germany, for example, and another in southern Texas. In both instances, Dobler identifies with the personae. "I could hear it breathing . . ." she says, presumably of Munich, "the old city, simmering under the new" and ends on a note of personal distress, having discovered that here "Everyone looks like me." Observing the tarantula shedding his skin she is suffused with admiration, or longing: "To have a new body. . . . To slip out of your body, to drop it like an old shirt."

Surely there will be more experimentation, more evidence of travel in the next book. But no one has more aptly noted, loved and forgiven a father than this poet, writing of his aphasia:

> . . . because now you think "death"
> but say "black feather," here is a garden:
> pass your hand over the face of this thing you've
>   forgotten,
> this "flower." Whatever you name it, so it will be.
> Hello or Forgive Me. I Loved You. Good-bye.

Maxine Kumin
1986 Judge
Brittingham Prize in Poetry

Acknowledgments

Magazines in which the following poems appeared, at times in different versions or with different titles, are:

The Bellingham Review, "Carolyn at 20"
Black Warrior Review, "The Mill in Winter"
Cape Rock, "How to Winter Out"
Crosscurrents, "What Mother Wanted for Me"
Hanging Loose, "Family Traits," "Separations"
Kayak, "False Teeth," "Uncles' Advice," 'Steelmark Day Parade, 1961," "Brother Plans to Move," and "I Get Jealous of an Old Home Movie"
Intro 12, "Carolyn at 16," "The Rope"
The Laurel Review, "Cold Frame"
The Ohio Review, "Jealous Wife," "August," "Paper Dolls"
Poet and Critic, "Father on the 40-Meter Band"
Poetry Northwest, "Alternate Universe," "1066"
Poetry Now, "Family Dream"
Prairie Schooner, "Book Circle," "The Ghost," "Two Photographs"
Sun Dog, "Carolyn at 40"
Tar River Poetry, "Steel Poem, 1912"
Tendril, "World Without End"
Three Rivers Poetry Journal, "1920 Photo"

"The Rope" was anthologized in *Saturday's Women* (Saturday Press, 1982); "Carolyn at 16" was anthologized in *The Best of Intro,* 1985. "Carolyn at 20" received a Pushcart Prize and is reprinted in *The Pushcart Prize, VIII: Best of the Small Presses.* "World Without End" received an AWP Anniversary Award in 1984.

Some of these poems were published in *Annex 21:* American Poetry Series, Vol. IV, 1982 (University of Nebraska Press: Omaha).

I wish to thank the Corporation of Yaddo, the National Endowment for the Arts, and the Pennsylvania Council on the Arts for their generous support during the completion of this book.

Heartfelt thanks to Charlotte Mandel, whose sensitive editorial suggestions and generosity of spirit helped make this book possible.

I

Field Trip to the Mill

Sister Monica has her hands full
timing the climb to the catwalk
so the fourth-graders are lined up
before the next heat is tapped, "and no
giggling no jostling, you monkeys!
So close to the edge!" She passes out
sourballs for bribes, not liking
the smile on the foreman's face,
the way he pulls at his cap,
he's not Catholic. Protestant madness,
these field trips, this hanging from catwalks
suspended over an open hearth.

Sister Monica understands Hell
to be like this. If overhead cranes clawing
their way through layers of dark air
grew leathery wings and flew screeching
at them, it wouldn't surprise her.
And the three warning whistle blasts,
the blazing orange heat pouring out
liquid fire like Devil's soup
doesn't surprise her. She understands
Industry and Capital and Labor,
the Protestant trinity. That is why
she trembles here, the children clinging
to her as she watches them learn their future.

Your Language Is Lost at Sea

Since you didn't speak their language
and besides were scared of the big Russian girls
with their oiled black hair and coarse gestures,
silence became your sister, she kept everything
in her heart, in the chill dark, in the hold
of your ship bound for the new country.
Silence was the chosen one in whose deep lap
you buried the Hunkie gutturals and sibilants,
keeping back only the few consonants and vowels
you thought your children would need in Ohio.
So your story trickles down the years: "Say nothing
if you are hungry, tired, poor. And wish to be
nothing as your syllables fall, break the ocean's skin.
With empty hands touch your body,
its boundaries and frontiers. Whoever invades,
hold tight, hold your tongue. Silence will bless
like a sister the tears you keep to yourself."

The Rope

Their voices still wake me
as I woke for years to that rise and fall,
the rope pulled taut between them,

both afraid to break or let go.
Years spilled on the kitchen table,
picked over like beans or old bills.

What he owed to the mill, what she wanted
for him. Tears swallowed and hidden
under layers of paint, under linoleum rugs,

new piled on old, each year the pattern
brighter, costlier. *The kids*
he would say, *if it weren't for*

She'd hush him and promise
to smile, saying *This is what*
I want, this is all I ever wanted.

My Father's Story

The blast furnaces dead, the cities dark,
the iron and ice ringing underfoot
but ringing for nothing, all for nothing,
no light in any house but kerosene,
the Depression a huge fact, a frozen hump
he couldn't get over or around,
the primitive helplessness
of his parents—outraged,
the young man leaves to cut
ice on the pond, 40¢ an hour,
his bucksaw biting deep
into another man's property.
If he can't shape steel
he will sheathe these blocks
in yellow sawdust and lay them up
against the coming heat.
The ice at least will have
its occupation: in July, sweating
his sweat, oozing its wet golden drops
onto the ice house floor.

Steel Poem, 1912

for Kevin

When the mill crept into his bunkroom
beating a fist on his wall

and the sun rose in sulphur
piercing the company house

he dressed with the men
cursing the lard on his bread

the sponge of new steel
waiting for him and his brothers

the shovel and pound
the steel rolling out

and he dreamed of dovehunting
plump birds hanging like fruit

the soft bones eaten with flesh
how they tempered the heart of the eater.

1920 Photo

Here is Grandpa, who did not want America,
flanked by children, wife and brother,
brother's wife and children. . . . Standing
to one side, a Chinese woman.

How did she get into this picture!
My mother can't, none of my aunts
can tell me, but they are children here,
see their rosy faces. The mustachioed men,
their women proud in white lace blouses,
a solemn occasion . . . and the Chinese woman

in a stiff bright robe, her eyes shining
into mine. Except for her, everyone touches
everyone else, all of them are making it
in America, even if Grandpa cries for Hungary
at harvest-time, even if he is a landless farmer
who shovels slag at the rolling mill.

Even the Chinese woman, who no one alive remembers,
who migrated into my family's picture
like a jungle bird among chickens,
looks happier to be here than Grandpa.

Family Traits

1.
Always one last order
before she released them
from their oven-on-wheels,
the family Ford:
Don't ask for anything.

The children never questioned this.
Their mother's pride was at stake.
They knew better than to wish out loud
for a cold Royal Crown or ice cream,
and if offered anything
even Aunt Mary's noodle pie
they knew how to refuse.

They practiced refusal
sitting on the prickly sofa
watching bars of buttery light
through the Venetian blinds,
feeling brave while their mother's sisters
begged them to eat a little something,
but not relenting until they saw
their mother's discreet nod.

As grown-ups, they notice their hands
are often groping and empty
but they only know how to refuse
and they're still not asking for anything.

2.
At Grandpa's wake my uncles sit together,
waiting to be fed. Not speaking yet.
They rest their arms on the long table,
rounding their shoulders under stiff white shirts.

When words come, you out there will hear
only the economy of their sentences:
"That goddam choir." "The Old Man
loved fiddle-music for dancing, you know, *czardas*,
so when Johnny dumped his fiddle on the B&O tracks . . ."
"We should have learned Hungarian, but we got our faces
    slapped
if we didn't talk American." "No matter what he said,
I never talked back." "That damned young priest,
couldn't even say the Old Man's name right."

My uncles share a habit they picked up
from the Old Man: whenever they lose their tempers
they bite their tongues. Today they nearly
bite their tongues in two, hooking the teeth
in the thick dumb muscle
that jerks in their mouths like a bludgeon.

False Teeth

Walking back to her sister's house,
woozy from relief and Novocain,
she nearly trips on the B&O tracks.
Then she sees it. A $20 bill.

Not crumpled. Folded between the ties,
pleated into a little fan, as if arranged
by whatever tooth fairy looks after
30-year old women who lose all their teeth.

When she walks into her sister's and grins,
she scares the baby—her swollen face,
the gums still bleeding, her words clotted
like the cries of an animal—

They think she's gone crazy with pain until
she holds up the money. The men are laid off
again, but she can pay the dentist
what he's owed, she can buy false teeth.

They say, "For every child, a tooth,"
and this is a story for children
whose toothless mother lost
and found and came out even.

Uncle Rudy Explains the Events of 1955

We laid the last course of firebrick
in the big 3-storey kiln when something broke upstairs.
Us brickies on the kiln bottom held our breath
at the first whiff of lime, we knew that stuff
could blind you, burn your lungs.
Each man found another man's hand
before shutting his eyes, so we inched out
that way—like kids, eyes shut tight
and holding hands. Climbed the ladder, finally up
to sweet air, the lime falling like snow
and burning our skin all the way.
That was the winter I found a rabbit
in one of my traps still alive.
The noise he made. "Quit it quit it quit it."
Lord, just like a person. So I quit.

August

Someone hung bronze bells on the saplings
growing from the cellarhole

at the edge of Mr. Bryant's cornfield.
They rang a little, company to locusts

who filled each cave of trees, a choir
I could step into, walking down the road,

or out of, if I chose. Better
to sit in dust, under the arbor,

pulling down hollyhock blossoms.
Mother lay in the house,

bearing down. My sister's head emerged,
a purple plum. She wore her skin

so like the hollyhock dolls
mother had made all summer:

the blossom a full-skirted gown,
the head a green bud, skewered
by a single straight pin.

Paper Dolls

Shoeboxes full of them, so helpless
yet haughty, mascaraed eyes
open and distant; the cardboard bodies,
naked except for wisps of peach lingerie,
not like our mother's body, zippered in smocks.

How we made the dolls bow,
imagining the rustle of dresses,
murmuring the names
which were not like our names:
Giselle. Martine. Katrinka.

They could not speak. We spoke for them,
exchanging identities like spies,
settling marriages and dowries,
folding them in outfits labeled "Tennis."
"Lunching at Maxim's." "Caribbean Sail."

We moved into their bodies, divided
the males among us. Until our mother
called us down to set the table,
we could live anywhere, eat what pleased us,
wear electric blue satin and furs.

All Souls Day, 1957

This is the day the poor souls wait for,
it is Christmas to them.
We run into church and out,
saying our prayers aloud and fast,
every set of prayers a ransom
breaking another soul free
from Purgatory's swampy floor.

Slipping between the brass doors,
black uniforms flapping about our knees,
we are raucous crows, but no one stops us.
Spirits drift up to Heaven like soap bubbles,
borne by our Paters and Aves, or by the draft
from the constantly opening doors.

All day, we are diligent about this work:
in the dawn before Mass, during recess,
after school, until the air turns blue
with burning leaves, for so many thousands
of souls are lined up like paratroopers
aimed upwards, poised for a hundred,
a hundred thousand years, waiting
for our prayers to cut them loose.

This is the day we are powerful:
not Sister or Father, not even God Himself
can say no to us, as we command that a murderer
(one who repented before the switch was thrown)
may put by his pain and soar.
Even the atheist Russians must envy us
as their Sputnik circles our little world
and their dog presses his nose to the window
watching our poor souls enter Paradise.

Lessons

Aunt Julie's hands knot and whiten
as she squeezes cucumber slices
handful by small handful
into the pale green bowl.

Called away from the uncles
to help in her hot kitchen,
I am beginning to learn
the woman's part. The man's part

is no better. After his mill shift
Uncle Vernon will stand at the back door,
shaky and black. He likes

cucumber salad, so this is the least
Aunt Julie can do: wringing the slices
as if they are somebody's neck.

The Mill in Winter

Below them, the valley cradles
the mill's dark body which lay
for a decade like a stunned animal,
but now awakens, almost innocent again
in the morning light. A pale disk of sun
pinks the crusted snow the men walk on,
the first thin columns of smoke brush the sky,
and the odors of coke and pickling acid
drift toward them. They taste metal on their tongues
and yearn toward the mill's black heart.
To enter, to shut out the bright cold air
is to enter a woman's body, beautiful
as ashes of roses, a russet jewel,
a hot breath grazing their arms and necks.

Uncles' Advice

My handsome uncles like dark birds
flew away to war. They all flew back
glossier and darker than before, but willing
to be clipped to the mill for reasons
of their own—a pregnant girl,
a business failed, the seductive sound
of accents they'd grown up with—
so they settled, breaking promises to themselves.
This was the time I moped in my room
while the aunts' voices rose through the floorboards
prophesying my life, stews and babushkas.
But the uncles' advice also filtered up
like the smoky, persistent 5-note song
of the mourning dove: get out, don't come back.

Carolyn at 16

Mama and Nana hide behind
the front porch, whispering *money*
money as you swing on the porch
like a ship into Sex Ocean with your slick
exchange student from Ecuador.

His elegant feet flick the porch boards
quick as a lizard's tongue. And his shirt
fluorescing under the street light, white on white!
The living room sighs with applause
for you, honey loaf—the family's capital.

The old women click like sticks
in the tiny rooms stuffed with rosewood,
they trace circles on the wet rims
of old crystal. You on the porch swing,
meant to restore their nice world,

Carolyn, your black hair cloudy, lifting
from your neck in the humid air—
marriageable, he thinks, *virgin*,
but not rich, not *católica*,
and flips his cigarette over the rail.

Carolyn at 20

One hand on the trailer door, one holding
your baby, you turn to watch the oilrag sun
swipe down the sky. All Middletown knows
the father: string-muscled briarhopper
your mama says you *chose*; and he's decamped.

You sit like a stump outside town
or hang out the diapers like flags;
you bury the trailer wheels in cement sockets,
oh thorn in your mama's side. Judgment,
she says, that gray streak in your glossy hair,

but standing under the fuming sky,
your son's fist in your hair, you name it:
joy, the dark rooms of your mother's house
exploded at last, the caverns of a man's body
shot with light, as beautiful as you suspected.

Carolyn at 40

When she leaves his house the sun bruising her skin
hurries her toward the car, the safety of leather,
the notebooks clotted with specs
of the "homes" she tries to sell.

Leaning into the car mirror, she pushes back
a stiff wing of hair the same sure way
she pushed his head back, baring his throat.
He's not much older than her son.

Carolyn shuffles photos of ranches
and handy-man specials, dealing them
like tarot cards: the farm means *love*,
the condominium means *you'll never go back*.

Brochures spill to the floorboards.
She crushes one, wiping her hands
of his body's lingering scent.
It's late, she has to get out of here.

What Mother Wanted for Me

What then do I want?
A life in which there are depths
beyond happiness. . . .
                    —Louis Simpson

A house like hers, nicer
but not so nice as to be strange.
Richer sooner. Younger longer.
More of my teeth in my head.

A man like hers but
no midnight turns. No layoffs
or salt tablets for the heat, no milk
for the ulcer. No accidents.

Children. Not so many.
Love that would know
how to make a bed and lie in it,
no complaints. Love that could eat

whatever was put on its plate
or stand before its gravesite
and stare without flinching at the stone
long before it carried dates.

Steelmark Day Parade, 1961

Blondes are everywhere—on floats,
watching from sidewalks, blond cops
joking with tow-headed kids, pale
high school bands with glinting horns.
My dark-haired visitor from Chicago
asks if the town exposes brunettes at birth,
and what we have done with our Negroes.

The strawberry, copper and yellow hairs
on everyone's heads blur in the sun,
doubling and tripling the flash
of steelmarks stamped everywhere
on the floats just passing from view.
This steelmark is heraldic, new,
a steel-blue brand honoring the men
who make steel. Everyone loves it.

"But really, where *are* the Negroes?"
he asks again. Not here, not yet,
they don't exist in 1961. Even the word
Black lies hidden in old wood houses,
cooped in dim regions between the railroad tracks
and the Pentecostal church, forbidden
to make steel or wear the steelmark
branded on the hardhats of the town's blond men.

Consumers

Suddenly they were all rich.
Pickups bloomed with trailer hitches,
outboard motors shone in the driveways.
They'd convoy to the lake, swim and grill steaks
until the men left for 4 to 12's.

Daily, the women had
something new to talk about,
but the chromed machines
purring in their kitchens
and the strangeness of old rooms
masked with stiff brocade
unnerved them; frowning, they fingered
drapes and carpets like curators.

They began to pack fat onto bellies and thighs
as if preparing for a long journey on foot
through a frozen country, a journey
they would have to take alone and without provision.

Brother Plans to Move

If he can choose, he'll dance out of town,
his wife tossing her hair, gold earrings
down to her shoulders catching the light,
his children robed in scarves like flames,
all of them in carnival masks, tossing pennies
to the stay-at-homes, and it won't matter
when bits of the mill struggle for breath and stir
and mutter after them as they wheel out of town.
They'll slap the dust from their sandals
on the "Welcome to Middletown" sign.
If they look back, the town will turn to salt.

Your Idioglossia

for my sister

Our private language had to stop,
I can see that now, they had to
separate us—you to speech therapy,

me to wait for you in the cobbled yard
without toy or book, watching
the water's slow drip from fountain

to stone basin where the orange carp
flashed and retreated. I understood
it was my fault no one understood

a word you said, but I was glad to keep you
in our puzzle of language, I was keeper
of your tongue—our parents had to

find the door, knock, *ask* to be let in.
Do you remember any of those words?
Sometimes odd syllables swim up and I catch

a glimpse of bright enameled scales,
the pure verb, a long muscle of orange—
then water closes over my head.

Family Dream

I am rolling around on the big bed with Uncle
Jimmy. It's ok, it's only sex, the rest
of the family crowds into the bedroom, laughing
about new babies, new wine. "Bulls Blood"
says Uncle Rudy. Suddenly I remember:
only two lbs. of lamb in the kitchen,
to feed so many! I run down to the kitchen,
start cubing the lamb for goulash.
Mother comes in and tells me to do
something with noodles. "More lamb!" I say.
"Send a cousin out for lamb."
"And who will pay?" asks Mother.

We gaze at each other.
This is a money matter, this is serious
business. I wake up, ravenous.

After Watching a Film about Cargo Cultists

Like everyone else, they want to be happy,
have simply confused cause with effect.
They surmise that
if you build airports you get goods:
cartons of canned soup, boxes of music, pictures that talk;
so they spend their days not working for wages
but in contriving sham runways
marked with bits of bark and paper lanterns
meant to lure the American god,
the giver of gifts, down from the sky.

In the movie the men stand with hands enmeshed
in the wirelink fence surrounding
one of our army's airports, a look of longing
on their faces as they gaze at our planes,
a look I've seen before on faces
in Ohio shopping malls, at family reunions
when the California cousins pass around photos
of white yachts on blue water. . . .
a shared belief that somewhere
in the guts of expensive machines
lives that soft animal, peace-of-mind.

How to catch and keep it
is the problem, how to fool the god
so he'll descend and be captured,
so the soul residing in the roar of the new
power mower or in the twinkle
of the swimming pool's blue eye
will enter the faithful
like the Pentecost dove
blessing and burning
transforming the world.

Grandma's Hands

She flattened my hand on the table,
teaching me loss. Castle Kamen assembled
again under her tracing fingers:
here, the footbridge arched over a troll
who beckoned her, having lured
the soul of her sister, dead at eighteen,
a blank of braids and white dresses;
there, the dining room trembled; the hungry ghost
beat her little shoes against the shelves,
the crockery swayed, "but when we look,
is nobody there." And the chicken run
soaked with blood, where her father
levelled his gun at gypsy women, laughing
as they dropped fat hens from under
their full skirts—over all these fallen places
she shook lost harvest smells,
the sweet Hungarian pepper.

Days in her Ohio kitchen, in the ordinary rooms
where tables hid in oilcloth, in her garden
where St. Francis smirked among white-painted rocks,
her hands gave shape to the air.
Her crooked fingers,
one thumb nail-less from a parrot's bite,
made me yearn for another world
that breathed in roots of the grass not here,
not in Ohio where nothing ever happened.

II

The Persistent Accent

> Until the grave covers me,
> on foreign soil
> I shall remain Hungarian.
> —Hungarian folk song

Because this fat old lady
has exactly the voice
of my dead grandma,
I find myself
trailing her through the supermarket
as she complains to her friend
about the Blacks, the kids, the prices,
age, disease, and certain death,
and I'm seduced
by that Hungarian accent
decades in this country can't diminish,
and I see the smoky fires
of the harvesters, a golden-braided girl
fetching their dinners of peppers and lamb,
and I follow her
through the aisles,
wanting to lay my face
between her hands,
to ask her for a song.

Father on the 40–Meter Band

At peace again, the company upstairs,
my father sits in his basement flicking switches.
Triangular dials glow obediently green
as the stacks of receivers and transmitters,
sheathed in gray metal, stutter to life.

Bunched wires furred with dust may seem
to spring like anarchy from the backs
of his machines, but that is illusion:
he is in control, his hands soldered the wires
and planted the tall antenna for catching voices.

Soon he will call "CQ" into the night,
and a stranger will answer.
"Do you read me? How's my signal?"
All afternoon my father suffered his family,
the stories of their lives. He does not care

for stories, he is interested in signals
clear or faint, anyone's voice homing in
over the miles. Upstairs, I watch
the herringbone pattern of his voice
on the TV: my father, talking to strangers.

Jealous Wife

1

We built the house with a blank wall
facing north: no openings for storms
or winter wind. I want to live
like that wall, blind to how you see yourself,
or be the dead and shining moon,
swollen hunter's moon in the bare elm,
or even less: shadows cast on a kitchen window.

2

Here lies the full skeleton of a deer.
You hope the hunter dropped him
with one shot, though you know
it didn't happen that way.
The delicate puzzle of footbones,
precise as a map, tells you
he climbed here to die.
You pity the animal who dragged himself
into this alder stand.
But everything reduces to sexual bones:
gates that swing open, glittering, underground.

3

Bad dreams, bad dreams, a woman outside
points to our door, but it is locked.
The red chair holds me in a stiff arm,
smoke rises under the lampshade, my hand
unravels the light gathered in a wineglass.
This is fear, it should be anger,
my face should rise like the moon,
searching outside, the policeman's beam
shining into your car.

Finding My Twenty-Year-Old Chicago Diary

1

In the middle of my life I can
look down time's tunnel and find her,
but I can't grab her by the hair
and shake her free from the desk where she works
or writes in her secret journal
when she should be working,
or gazes at the lake "striated like the muscles
on a man's back." She is newly married,
still wonders at sex,
there is no way for me to save her.
She wants poetry and "ordinary human happiness"
and is still young enough to believe
she can have both at once.

2

She watches Lake Michigan freeze solid
ninety-six miles across, the ice green
but sometimes "mimicking the air's no-color,
the waves frozen in attitudes as if about to break."
She is about to break, and I want her back
so I can put my hands again
on the thin cold face that lived in my mirror.
I'd be her good mother before her babies come
and croon a lullaby about giving over
to the wind, bending like the trees
she writes of, bent along the Outer Drive,
their wind-flattened, squat, but vivid forms
an image to her as she bends over her proofsheets:
Adventures in Reading: A Teacher's Manual, Grade 5.

3

Her husband rises, dresses in the dark,
leaves their building eating an apple,

his teeth cracking into white flesh:
delight in the crack of the icy
train platform under his feet.
Under the frozen lake the swelling water
prepares to break free and he plants his feet
on the surface of a world which will yield
to him and to the wife he left in bed
with proof her body is good for something—
he felt the child fluttering
under her skin, the work between them.
She is willing to pay for her choice
while the surge of another life, like the lake
tossing its bones, buries the words deep under:
"*plain* is a good word, and so is *smear*."

4

As morning comes on, things resume their lives:
the lake leaves the arms of the dark air
and steps once more into its own shape,
trees detach from rocks, mother and daughter part.
Each thing in the dense world of things
says hello to itself, delighted to be
in the light again. But for her the only way out
is down, through black water. If she holds her breath
for fifteen years, she is still living a life,
a body becomes history for the children,
a rib around which their lives accrue,
for in the lived life, nothing is final.
By entering the lake weighted on both hips
she can walk the bottom,
allowing the lake's heavy plate to press her down
until bitterness leaches from her and time lets her rise.

Separations

1
The last angry word hangs like a cleaver
over the shag carpet, then slices down,
and there is a ravine in the living room floor
dividing husband and wife who gape at each other
from either side.
        At the gulley's bottom
a thin line of horsemen, silent from this distance,
threads its way through pin-oaks and a desultory stream.

2
The tourists admire the ice floes; it may be
that we are also picturesque: a tired man
with a sore throat, two weeping children,
the seasick mother.
        Our captain says,
"We call it calving when the glacier splits."
And the ice hits the water
before we hear the sounds of that birth.

The Gazebo

Mr. Bryant built the gazebo
their first year together.
Shavings fell from his dovetail plane
blond as a young wife's curls.
He dreamed of her white skin
while the eaves curved under his hands,
and he trained the grape vines
to grow over the sides
and darken the open room.

Mrs. Bryant strung the washlines there,
after she retrained the vines
to grow on a proper arbor.
A gazebo's a good place for laundry
when it rains, and it rains
most of the summer, in Vermont.

I Get Jealous of an Old Home Movie

How sharply I catch my breath—
his movie of Christina skating
red hair flying
as she drifts
among the dead trees
studding the frozen pond,
a fluent bird alive
in the still trunks and branches.
Those images are acid flung in my face
by Jealousy, that useless hag,
who after all these years
can still catch me under the ice
and tie my hair
to the roots of frozen trees
while Christina's skates
cut the ice above me,
indifferent and free.

Hospital Call

The angel hunching on the TV set is bored.
I won't look at her, but can feel
the irritated whirr of wings
as I lean over my husband,
watching his thick chest fill and fall,
letting his breath wash my face.
The angel's not waiting for him.
She wants the black man in the next bed,
the one with cold fingers
and no wife to stand over him and pray
the sweat to break from his body.

The angel visits so many rooms like this one—
fluids pumping into bodies, pumping out,
nightsweat and vomit, dank hair spread on pillows—
she likes this taking to be easy.
She wants us to be beautiful and good,
cool as white nightgowns carved in stone.

I want a barroom brawl,
the TV blaring the Steelers score,
the black man banging his glass,
poking his finger in my husband's chest,
while I pull out
the angel's cotton candy hair
by its black roots.

The Ghost

In the darkness my husband could sense it
standing at the foot of the bed, hunched
and hesitant. Then the small sound
of a hand touching coins on the dresser.
"What do you want? Go away!" he said.
He wasn't afraid, just firm, and the sternness
in his voice woke me from a dream:

A woman had wandered onto a road
and was lost where no one wanted her.
The hemlocks pressed her close on either side,
their black hands laced, so she needed
to keep moving toward the one figure
she could see, outlined in light:
a man waving impatiently from the road's crown,
his voice imperious, demanding something.

After the Facts Came Out

Ellen R., the gourmet cook
who secretly melted her flesh back to its bones
must have hated us as we stuffed ourselves
on her marriages of butter and egg,
sweetbreads in velvet sauce,
raspberry hearts melting with sugar.
At table she sat upright watching us eat
her celebrated bouillabaise; she shaved
dark chocolate curls for our delight,
and when we moaned with pleasure, she would smile.

But at the New Year's buffet
she lifted her long dress over her head—
the skimmed blue-white skin stretched over ribs,
the sharp-edged dish of pelvis, the two scraps
of breast, a presentation for the dinner guests.
Not long after, she left her husband, gave up cooking,
went back for her Ph.D. and the life of the mind.

Book Circle

In February, in Ramona's house
with its authentic stencilled walls,
they gathered to discuss
Charles Williams' Anglican ghost stories.
Meanwhile, little sexual brushfires
caught all over the room.
The cold Vermont wind swept under the hall door,
they drew close to the fireplace
and turned to the story in which a woman
meets her Doppelgänger in Cambridge. . . .
and a man changes into lion, serpent, bear. . . .
"Marriage is a burning house,"
Ramona told her guests. All of them
were married, but not to anyone present.
Ramona's voice sounded against the windows,
black diamonds against the night sky.
One of the guests knew she shouldn't be there,
and pulled on her thick gloves. A wasp
which had crawled into a glove gave the sting,
something for her to carry back home.

On Murray Avenue

I don't know the boy who runs
toward me, holding out his arms.
You look so pretty, he shouts,
and grabs me round the shoulders.
I see that only his mind
is young—some mother's hand
still combs his hair, though it's graying,
but maybe he chose the red tee-shirt,
it looks brand-new, and if
my heart were less a closed fist
I would not shudder
out of this sidewalk two-step,
I'd hug him back, tell him
he looks pretty too.

The Golden Ox Cafe

A newspaper clipping from home, headlined
"Duke Morris—Tough Guy, Poetry Lover."

Morris owns and runs
The Golden Ox Cafe in Dayton Ohio.
An ex-boxer, ex-Marine.

He says, "I love poetry
final and foremost in my life.
I love poetry more than I do women."

———————————

A friend, a notable writer, got drunk
at my house, lay down on the floor
and cried, "I have no spiritual life."
Then he said he had no character,
for he could not bear to leave his wife
although he loved another woman
and longed to be with her.

———————————

Duke Morris believes his poetry
will catch on in a big way once he has died
and will make him immortal.

"I don't want any money," Morris said.
"I don't want to be rich.
"I want everyone to read my poems."

———————————

The notable writer thinks that when he is 80
he will be happy again, for then
no one will care who he fucked, only what he wrote.
He thinks of poems extending themselves,
thickening like the rich vines of honeysuckle
behind his mistress' house, and sex

as just a metaphor for writing, and on this point
Duke Morris would probably agree.

———————————

The man who loves poetry more than women
is coming to terms in Ohio, in The Golden Ox Cafe,
wiping down vinyl tables, upending chairs.

He draws the shades, eats some leftover
stew and bread, sets out his workbook
with its marbled cover, picks up his favorite pen.

I'm Calling the Exterminator

I don't know how the raccoon broke into the chimney
but I want it out: alive, dead, whole or in pieces,
poisoned, shot or merely discouraged from its anxious
    scrape scrape scrape
at 3 A.M. in the chimney's hollow behind my headboard.
Imagine its clever worried mask, the quick paws
passing over each other, clawing a space in my life
when I'm helpless and asleep, the stubborn scrabbling of
    the creature
no matter how hard I hit the wall with the baseball bat—
what can it be doing back there? I hear drawers opening
    and closing,
furniture dragged along the floor then dropped. Then,
    muffled curses.

How to Winter Out

Love the land mass, the enclosure
of a continent around you.
Think of yourself as the hot center.

Remember frostbite, how the blood rushes
from hands and feet to save the heart.
Do likewise, pare down to the vital.

Do without color, except the necessary
cardinal on a branch,
a spot of blood on snow, a burning coal.

But dream when you sleep, and dream in color.
Do not tell your lover your dreams
unless he asks. Then embroider.

Otherwise, do not adorn. Make love
without speaking, make love in Spanish,
speak in tongues, but use no names.

German Stories

1
Fallen trees, their great trunks fluid with years,
sprawl among the brush and fireweed
or bend as girls do, brushing their hair.
I thrust my hand into a hollow tree
and draw out its sacred name,
the name we must never pronounce,
before the German machine, bristling with order,
comes to scour the woods it loves so much.

2
Early morning
waiting alone on the platform
mist rolling in
as if the past
were a door left open
waiting for the Munich train
its sleek body
enormous windows hiding nothing
no slatted sliding doors
a man's heavy tread
coming up the station steps
he whistles an old marching song

3
A Letter from Munich
Our landlady is kind to me and the children for we look Ger-
man. Also, I like to walk across the kitchen floor barefoot for
the pleasure of the scrubbed bleached wood under my feet.
The landlady knows this. Yesterday she taught me to make
plum tarts. We filled the kitchen with the smells of preserves
and burnt sugar. She said the Jews are *Fliegen,* and are best
dealt with—smack!—like *this.*

4

Cats live in the eternal present,
they have no internal clock,
they are like God.

Or like Germans, who have many clocks,
all of them external,
all of them on time,

many of them beautiful, like cats.
Like cats, they have no history,
have always stood on shelves

in shops with drawn curtains
where I stand now with the shopkeeper.
We sway back and forth like figures

on his cloisonne clock. Hansel and Gretel
shuffle on the witch's threshhold
while the cat's black tail swings: Tick, Tock.

5

The sudden apparition in the car mirror of a dark Mercedes-
Benz bearing down on us, 80, 90 mph?—headlights blink-
ing, then around us and gone. *What's happening?* My friend
laughs and smooths the feathers on his loden hat. "We are
not used to speed limits in Germany—when they put some
limit on the *Autobahn,* this was to us a life without joy, a
terrible burden, it depressed the whole nation. It's different
for Germans, we can't be constrained."

6

I could hear it breathing
under the streets, shackled

like a bad dog—the old city,
simmering under the new.
Yesterday a little woman
jostled me in Marienplatz.
I wanted to tear out her throat.
That's the trouble with this country,
its lack of distance,
and not enough faces.
Everyone looks like me.

Two Photographs

Why am I crying over these pictures?
My mother is alive,
my daughter is a beautiful young woman.
But here, each of them
is four again, with the same
soft chin and pale hair, even the same
nervous tic: five fingers stuffed in the mouth.
The feathery wisps of Lisa's hair,
a fragrance like cut grass
rising from Mother's neck. . . .
When Lisa burrowed in my arms,
my pleasure was the same as it was
for Mother when I shoved myself into her,
all those soft arms and legs twined round.
Lisa pretended to sleep so I would carry her
from car to bed, and I dreaded the time
she would not want to pretend.
I remember Mother's hand on mine,
tracing the storybook words
long after I knew their meanings,
and now I wish to hear whatever story
makes them look so sad in these pictures.
What can I do with this longing for that union,
touching their faces, then my own.

Cold Frame

March again, so we pry the cold frame open.
The hinged lid creaks like a knee,
but will hold together one more year.
As we shovel peat moss and clean sand,
I warn my daughter: not too rich a mixture,
or the roots grow shallow.
We pack the light loam down,
her fingers are longer than mine.
She is thirteen and careful
of her breasts, yet has a new way
of rocking back on her heels, like a woman.
As she listens, she plants the seed
in perfect rows; her gray eyes measure
the gaps in the cold frame, measure me.

May Morning

to WCW

Flick, flick, there his line goes again
over the backyards of Pittsburgh:
my neighbor practices flycasting,
leans from his second-story porch,
just misses the tangle of last year's nests
and the peeved sparrows as he spins out the thread,
flirting it over the green bushy banks
where imaginary trout lurk and flash,
hanging in pools under the peony bushes—
oh mingle of hope and desire, fish of our dreams—
while in the backyard burns
that green-broken-bottle color,
deep as the sea, and the scent
of our three brown rivers wafts
over the *sempervivum*, those little
cabbage plants, round as roses.

1066

A great wind, and a voice within the wind:
bed and window, house and child.
A voice hoards the old tongue,
a stone falls into the body's pond:
husband, sleep, north and west.
The fired huts, a blond man buries
bread and welcome, fire and hearth,
heaven and earth, bird and tree.
The old words freeze inside the throat
until love or death melt them
and out they flow, brighter than chivalry,
each word a drop of blood:
bloom knife summer friend.

So come Normans, and come servant
mantle convent feast venison and spice,
come guile and courtesy, come rich come poor,
come change delay escape, come doubt
and villain, chalice, rent and savory.
For a voice is singing to itself
under cliff, under grass:
thrive and thrust, gasp and want,
bride meadow beast bower
loom and stream. Happy or ill,
wise or weak, in full day
or skulking night the deep words rise:
path and way, beginning, end.

Forget Your Life

for Michele Murray, 1933–1974

Forget your life, it's familiar,
a housedress you've grown into
so that it seems your second skin.

Soon, pain will take you by the wrist
down to the river, where your skin
under the sloughed-off dress is fresh again.

Though you have rocked the child today
"for hours . . . and could not write,"
poems like cells divide under your breasts.

Soon, your poems will walk on their own,
holding up lanterns
as you enter the sliding river.

Alternate Universe

I can walk into the rain, turn the corner
at Fifth & Wood & vanish into something better,
something harder, a maple tree for example. . . .
Time curves in & out,
a train crawls along, hauling itself toward Juarez.
Or on a different train, the light slanted for winter
instead of July, what would he have said to me then?
I shake alternatives like snow in a glass globe
& the snow comes down, never the same way twice.
So, the train is bound for Juarez, now there's smoky gold
in the air, the cottonwoods shining, each leaf & stem
connected by a flat twist at the twig, the least wind
shakes the leaves, alternating gold & gray flashes,
but the leaves hold tight to their branches.
I'm dizzy from light brushed on leaves passing by,
the rainfall snowfall summer is quick to flame,
it settles into ash. He is far away,
the door spinning at the corner of Fifth & Wood
lets me enter his world where something else
might have happened at ground level. If I spin
the wheel again he might watch from his room my distant
     windows:
at sundown, each one blazes in turn, then darkens.

Tarantula

Nothing to see here but scrub, just a dirt road like a hot held
    breath
between El Paso and Chandelar, then in front of us,
a tarantula shedding his skin. In the grip of the one
    beautiful thing
he knows how to do.
The harmless and stout, the hairy and slow
tarantula leaving behind his replica,
exact to the last hair and spot.
This is hard work, he peels himself out, comes out soft and
    damp,
the pincers curved, pale ivory. Nothing
here but cactus, cholla that jumps at you, ocotillo like little
    whips,
still trembling, dropped from someone's hand. He could die
    now,
soft as he is. Watching him leave his body. To have a new
    body.
The distance between the shell turning to ash
and the tentative flex of his legs,
his slow walk away toward nothing we can see—
a line burning or the horizon, a thread of dust.
Heat carves the silence toward belief
in things unseen—this shroud of old skin
under my fingers.
To slip out of your body, to drop it like an old shirt.
To live, a tarantula must be hard and dry, and now he is,
and gone, blent into the pale dirt, gone before.

World without End

These insane layings of eggs by the thousands,
clear jellies clinging to the undersides of myriad leaves,
and in the streams and oceans, millions of clusters more,
the hordes eating their way southward through the trees,
or being eaten, but there's a plenty for food,
a plenty to live and breed more. Don't you tremble
at that fecundity? The mindless swell and burst,
and each like each like each. What kind of God desires
such multitudes. Stacked like cordwood on the streets in
    Delhi,
each a beloved soul. But oh
the raw cries of my father, the night his mother died.
My mother, who can see longer and harder than anyone,
now trying to ease him down. The deaths of the many
are nothing to me. When the sirens warn, I want
everyone I love gathered with me on a high mountain
where we start over, all of us saved by a miracle
because we are mild, intelligent and happy in our work.
But even God can't stop us
from standing on the quarry's edge, daring who will dive
into that black water first,
the insane laying of eggs, the thousands, the millions,
my father wrapped and dying in my mother's arms.

Aphasia

for my father

Because scared, because of *have to earn a dollar,*
because for every thing you earned, Grandaddy sat
on your shoulder saying "You're the lucky one,
if you fell into the shithole you'd come up
with a gold piece in your mouth," because traduced,
laughed at, lied to, because you trusted only your hands
and the perfect ribbons of steel rolling out of the mill,
because you never trusted words but filled a house
with the static of stockpiled things, every gadget,
every stick of furniture a barrier to the threat outside,
because you never felt at home in this world
of jokes and silences, because now you think "death"
but say "black feather," here is a garden:
pass your hand over the face of this thing you've forgotten,
this "flower." Whatever you name it, so it will be.
Hello or Forgive Me. I Loved You. Good-bye.

Dark Trail

I wasn't lost; no one could get lost
on such manicured trails, but without a moon
and caught between the party's and the house's lights
I stood inside the heart of a tree or maybe
inside the sky: I could have been suspended
anywhere, feet moving over—not on—
pine needles blowing down; whatever was left
between feet and head was probably
my body which ignited, a luminous raft,
a dream of flying or floating face down
hair adrift in the pool's gel.
It's good to die a little.
Nothing is taken away. If you and I
were together again on the paddle boat,
we could fly our dragon kite, letting it
follow the boat attached by the thinnest wire.
Lovely to tug on the line, to feel it strong,
tensed to break away. Pluck it,
you hear music higher than wind in these trees
burning their incandescent inward lights.

DESIGNED BY MIKE BURTON
COMPOSED BY G & S TYPESETTERS, INC.
AUSTIN, TEXAS
MANUFACTURED BY EDWARDS BROTHERS, INC.
ANN ARBOR, MICHIGAN
TEXT AND DISPLAY LINES ARE SET IN MERIDIEN

Library of Congress Cataloging-in-Publication Data
Dobler, Patricia.
Talking to strangers.
(The Brittingham prize in poetry)
I. Title   II. Series.
PS3554.0177T3   1986   811'.54   86-40046
ISBN 0-299-10830-9
ISBN 0-299-10834-1 (pbk.)